Did Grandpa's Dog Pass Gas?

Rita Ann Fleming

Illustrated by Abigail Marble

Spring & Maple Books LLC
Jeffersonville, IN

Illustrations © 2016 Abigail Marble. abigailmarble.com

First printing 2016

ISBN: 978-0-9864312-5-8
LCCN: 2016909978

ATTENTION CORPORATIONS, UNIVERSITIES, COLLEGES, AND PROFESSIONAL ORGANIZATIONS: Quantity discounts are available on bulk purchases of this book for educational, gift purposes, or as premiums for increasing magazine subscriptions or renewals. Special books or book excerpts can also be created to fit specific needs. For information, please contact Spring & Maple Books LLC, PO Box 1050, Jeffersonville, IN 47130.
DoesGrandmaHaveAMustache.com

DEDICATION

Thankful for John

Forty-two years...
"Who'd of thought?"

ACKNOWLEDGMENTS

Thanks to the resourceful staff at About Books, Inc.—
Debi, Scott and Larkin Flora, Cathy Bowman and Kaye Krassner
—for their enthusiastic support and expertise
in the making of this book.

Thanks to Abigail Marble for her amazing artistry.

Thanks to Bridgette, Jesse, Patrick, Josh and their families
"I really love my time with you.
Tomorrow..."

CONTENTS

CHAPTER ONE

Grandma and Grandpa I

Read Some More

"Oh goodness, Nick," my grandma said.
"An antenna's growing on top your head.
In the past two days, I've only seen
you stare into a TV screen.
So turn it off! Come read with me
another book of poetry."

Grandma's Glasses

Grandma searched in every room.
"I have to find my glasses soon.
Can't read a book or write a check
without my new prescription specs.
I know there's messages I've missed.
It's hard to make a grocery list.
Just recently I had a pair.
Now I don't find them anywhere."
I smiled at her. And then I said,
"Grandma, they're on top your head!"

Stuck

I had an awful craving for
a nutty caramel chocolate bar.
But when I put in fifty cents
my candy treat would not dispense.
I stretched my hand up through the slot,
and tried to reach and make it drop.
It's really stuck and just won't pass.
I'm mad enough to smash the glass.

Who's in charge of vending here?
It seems there is a faulty gear.
My grandma, passing by, just heard
me say a somewhat dirty word.
"It doesn't help for you to holler.
A candy bar now costs a dollar."
She added quarters, then we laughed.
I apologized, then gave her half.

Arbitrate an Allowance Rate

Dear Grandma,
I made this special card for you
with glitter, markers, stickers, glue.
I'd really like to send it with
a nice expensive birthday gift …
A necklace, ring, or diamond pin,
and jewelry box to put them in,
or extra glasses you could wear
(we know sometimes you need a spare).

But I find that now my funds are low.
I know how we could fix this, though.
Money doesn't grow on trees,
but maybe you could intercede.
Please talk to Mom and arbitrate
a generous allowance rate.
If she and Dad could be convinced,
I'll spend it on your new presents.

Love,
Nick

Grandma's Response

Dear Nick,

I'm grateful that you worked so hard
on my lovely birthday card,
and I admire your sweet intention
to buy the presents that you mentioned.
But as far as I'm concerned,
you save the money that you've earned.

The ideal gifts you give to me
are love, respect, and honesty.
Treat others by the Golden Rule.
Try to learn a lot in school.
And in addition to the list above
I'll always take a great big hug!

Love,
Grandma

Time for Games

My chores are done. Let's have some fun.
We start with Candy Land.
I pick a double purple card
and move my plastic man.

The next draw puts me in a swamp,
then on a licorice space.
Grandpa has the winning cards.
I finish in last place.

We next played Chutes and Ladders.
But every time I try,
I spin a losing number,
then down the board I slide.

We set up Operation.
This time I get to start.
I use the tweezers carefully
to lift a Broken Heart.

Grandpa nabs the Funny Bone
and Water on the Knee.
I have success with Spare Ribs,
but get the buzzer on Brain Freeze.

Parcheesi, Clue, or Cootie,
no matter what we choose,
despite my mighty effort
I continually lose.

I opt now for the Scrabble game.
I play this pretty well.
We sort out seven wooden tiles
and think of words to spell.

Luckily I pick a Z,
put ZEBRA on the board.
I have a Q, and then a U,
have QUIT on triple score!

My grandpa is impressed with me.
He's said so from the start.
"Unlike the other games we played,
this shows you're really smart!"

Colorful

If I'm healthy and happy,
I'll be in the pink.
If lonely or sad,
I'll feel blue.
If I'm scared half to death
I'll seem white as a ghost,
or look green if
I'm jealous of you.

But come Christmas season
I'll be my best color,
and do everything that I'm told,
so Santa will hear
when Grandma tells him this year,
"Our Nick, here, has been good as gold!"

Retired

Grandpa's retired. I'm not sure what that means.
But now he wears sweatshirts and sandals and jeans.

He's not rushing to work. We have more time to talk.
We go to the playground and walk in the park.

My grandma says he's now a jack-of-all-trades.
You wouldn't believe all the cool stuff he's made.

What you call it, I'm just mighty glad.
Retirement is more fun than we've ever had!

Fair Day Disaster

My grandma and grandpa, my sisters, and I
go to the fair every Fourth of July.
We headed to the food court. The smells were
    delicious!
"It's tasty," said Grandma, "but not quite
    nutritious."

We kids ate our corndogs all covered in mustard.
I spent my four dollars to buy frozen custard.
Grandpa and Sue ordered two funnel cakes.
Grandma and Clair drank their fresh lemon
    shakes.

My sisters and I nicely asked if we may
buy tickets for rides on the busy midway.
Clair mounted a horse on the merry-go-round.
Sue rode up the Freefall, then she fell straight
    down!

I flew on a coaster that ran lightning fast,
then stumbled off dizzy. "This ride is my last!"
"Time now," said Grandpa, "To take a few tries
at carnival games to each win a prize."

I knocked down some pins, got a bear for my mom.
My sisters had fun fishing in the duck pond.
Grandpa was proud of the T-shirt he won
shooting at targets with his BB gun.

"It's my turn," said Grandma. She looked for the stage
where a carny will guess at your weight or your age.
"How much do I weigh? Let's not speculate.
I gained a few pounds from that fair food I ate."

She dug through her purse, and found fifty cents.
"I'll win a prize. I've got confidence.
So try now, young man. My age? Can you guess?
I'm told I look younger by five years or less."

The man studied Grandma. "I estimate you
are not one day older than, say, sixty-two."
Grandpa tried bravely to hold back a laugh.
"Oh no," he said, "what a regrettable gaffe!"

Grandma was livid. "Now listen to me!
Young man, you need glasses. You clearly can't see.
Why not even close! And so out of line.
I'll have you know I have just turned fifty-nine."

She stomped out, exclaiming, "It's high time we go.
I've had quite enough of this sad, silly show."
Fair Day was fun, until that disaster.
Did Grandma have fun? I don't think I'll ask her!

Our Garden

Grandpa has a garden
and I'm the gardener's help.
Vegetables taste better
if they're ones I grow myself.

Beginning early in the spring
we start our seeds in pots,
then move them outdoors later,
'cause tomatoes like it hot!

We grow our beets and broccoli
(I pray we don't plant peas),
then cultivate our carrots,
and pull away the weeds.

It's hard work in the garden,
but all summer I'll keep trying.
To grow and eat my own food
I find really satisfying.

CHAPTER TWO

Critters

Did Grandpa's Dog Pass Gas?

An odd perfume had filled the room.
The family gathered all assumed
the culprit, with his eyes downcast,
was Grandpa's dog. Did he pass gas?

In unison, we all said "Phew!"
Did he acquire a stomach flu?
The odor seemed to flow downstream.
Perhaps he had a meal of beans.

The conversation all but ended.
Grandpa's dog looked quite offended.
He stared at me. He knew the truth,
'cause I had blown that mighty toot!

A Bit of Protein

Outside we were having fun
catching raindrops with our tongue.
I opened up my mouth and then
a buzzing insect flew right in!

I sputtered, stuttered, spit, and spewed.
Gagged until my face turned blue!
While I retched and choked and coughed,
the bug bit my esophagus!

I then proceeded to ingest him
in my small and large intestine.
I wondered, will he pass right through?
I asked my Grandpa what to do.

He said, "Well, this is not all bad.
It's a bit of protein that you had.
Crickets, ants, mealworms, grubs—
it's beneficial to eat bugs!"

Back to the Zoo

On Saturday while I was home
my grandpa called to ask,
"How about we see the zoo?
I'll use my senior pass."

We saw a docent just inside,
and asked him for directions.
"I'll walk with you a while," he said,
"in case you have some questions."

"Welcome," said the elephant.
"I'm quite sure we've met.
Your faces are familiar.
We tend to not forget."

The hyenas were hilarious.
They traveled in a pack.
"Tell us a funny joke," they begged,
"you know we love to laugh."

We saw the bats roost quietly.
They have meals at night.
"We eat mosquitos by the pound,
and sonar guides our flight."

We spied the baby kangaroo,
safe in his mother's pouch.
"I'm going to take a break," she said,
"this joey wears me out!"

The lion surveyed his kingdom.
We asked him, "Why so vain?"
"Who else, besides myself," he said,
"has such a gorgeous mane?"

"With due respect your highness,"
said a pair of chimpanzees,
"you might be king, but can you swing
for miles between the trees?"

The crocodiles were hungry.
They smiled and showed their teeth.
"We need these shiny canines
so we can chew our meat."

The aviary loomed ahead.
We stayed 'til well past two.
I liked the kookaburra
and the chatty cockatoo.

The vultures weren't selective.
"Leftovers? We don't mind.
We wait for scraps from predators,
and eat what's left behind."

We marveled at the eagle.
It made me sad to think
that this endangered species
almost became extinct.

It was getting dark outside,
we had stayed quite late.
Our friendly docent led the way
and took us through the gate.

On the way, while we walked home
I thought of all I'd learned.
I thanked my grandpa for the trip.
He said we'd soon return.

Kitten
Met His Match

Our once-courageous kitten
did become a fearless cat.
He ran off all those awful mice
and chased away a rat!

There's no crumb in the closet,
no droppings on the bed.
He rid us of the rodents
who were threatening my Ted.

But now it seems our fierce feline
has finally met his match.
He hides as quickly as he can
when Clair is on attack.

She puts him in her stroller,
makes him wear a little dress.
No longer free to roam alone,
the poor guy is distressed.

Our once-courageous kitten
has become a scared-y cat.
There's no doubt in our family
who's responsible for that!

Give That Liver Back

Mom served me a slice
of slivery liver.
I swallowed a sample.
My appetite withered.

It's really quite awful.
One bite was enough.
Who in the world
would savor this stuff?

I bet if you asked
the unfortunate cow
he'd undoubtedly say,
"Give my liver back now!"

Gerry or Geraldine?

Gerry my gerbil was still pretty sad.
He'd never bounced back from the trauma he had,
since he escaped and was found on the loose,
and had to endure Grandma's verbal abuse.

Recall that she thought he might be a raccoon.
His self-confidence was totally ruined.
Worse, she suggested, he could be a rat.
He was despondent, his affect was flat.

I finished my chores. I had money to spend.
I went to the store and bought Gerry a friend.
He's much more relaxed, not nearly as stressed.
Having a pal gives him much happiness.

He's perked up a lot, there's a gleam in his eye.
My once depressed pet is remarkably spry!
His bad attitude is a thing of the past.
He and his friend—they're having a blast!

"I'm glad," Grandma said, "that your pet's feeling great,
but I've recently noticed he's put on some weight.
There could be a reason that you might consider
why Gerry's developed a rather full figure.

"I'm pretty sure now that your pet Gerry may
be in what some call the 'family way.'
And I would suggest, due to facts unforeseen,
perhaps Gerry's name should become Geraldine."

Grateful Bait

Just like I was really wishing,
Grandpa said he'd take me fishing.
I opened up a can of bait,
then thought I heard a voice say, "Wait!"

A worm spoke up and begged of me,
"Please listen to my heartfelt plea!
Turn us loose and let us be.
We are one big family."

I looked at all his wormy kids.
They seemed as sad as their dad did.
They trembled when they took a look
at my pointy fishing hook.

"Okay," I said, "I'll spare you guys."
Then I tied on a plastic fly.
The grateful bait all slithered out,
then I caught a great big trout!

(But in case you need to know,
I also let that big trout go.)

Can't Take a Yak Back

Just once I wish the zoo would say,
"Adopt a critter for the day.
Take a bird or beast to borrow.
Bring him back by five tomorrow.
How about a newt or gnu?
A wallaby or kangaroo?
Perhaps a pelican or parrot,
flamingo, frog, or feisty ferret?"

I'd gather up a rope and net,
and pick a temporary pet.

I might choose a large baboon
to spend some time up in my room.
A polar bear or crocodile
could sunbathe in our pool awhile.
Would Mom be angry if I tell her
a lizard's living in our cellar?
Or a cockatoo who's charismatic
felt at home up in our attic?

I'll settle on a friendly yak.
But when I try to take him back,
the zoo might say, "He's just a spare.
We have too many—keep him there."
Do you think my parents would agree
to let this yak stay home with me?

CHAPTER THREE

School Days

A Pony "Tale"
Outside the Lines
SHHHHHH – Silent Letters
The "ph" and the "gh"
A Tasty Show and Tell
Careers
Anyone Can Be a Poet
Glasses
Sleeper
The Dog Ate My Homework (Really!)
Lousy Middle Name
Whatever

A Pony "Tale"

This girl who sits in front of me
takes up too much space.
She flips her ponytail all day
and twirls it in my face.

I asked her, twice, politely,
to move her head of hair.
I just can't learn my lessons
when her ponytail is there.

The last straw happened just last week.
I finally dropped my guard.
I grabbed that swinging ponytail
and yanked it rather hard.

The only thing that's worse
than my after school detention
is that she's telling all her friends,
"I like Nick's attention!"

Outside the Lines

My friend Alexander
insists on the rules
in art class where he really shines.

With utmost precision
and careful control,
he's careful to stay in the lines.

But I'll be a rebel!
No limits for me.
I choose to ignore the confines.

I purposefully try
when using my crayons
to color outside of the lines.

My friends will all whisper
and tattle on me.
(You'd think I'm committing a crime!)

I won't win a prize.
But I can't compromise!
And color inside of the lines.

SHHHHHH – Silent Letters

Knuckle, gnome, pneumonia--
are tricky words. Prepare!
Psychic, scissors, sandwich--
will catch you unaware.

Autumn, column, castle,
whether, wrist and rhyme--
Learn them well so you can spell
correctly every time!

TELEPHONE

PNEUM

WHETHER LAUGH

WRIST

PHRASE

COLUMN

SIGN

PHASE

PHLEGM

UE

ROROUGH

The "ph" and the "gh"

Beware! More tricky letters
will appear on spelling tests,
where the "ph" and the "gh"
can sound just like a "f."

There's telephone and pharmacy,
tough and rough and laugh,
alphabet, apostrophe,
phase, and paragraph.

So if those silent letters
aren't troublesome enough,
The "ph" and the "gh" words
are bound to trip you up!

A Tasty Show and Tell

Last week our health instructor asked
that we bring fruit to share in class.

Hannah brought bananas
and she peeled one just for me.
Jesse plucked a juicy apple
from his backyard tree.
Thomas made a promise
to share with us his pear.
Patrick's purple pomegranate
had lots of seeds—beware!
Harry purchased cherries
and his mother made a pie.

Chloe cried, "This kiwi's good.
Josh, give it a try."
"Have a cantaloupe," said Hope.
"I eat it every day."
Mary picked blueberries
and served them with sorbet.
Lucy sliced a lemon.
She made a sourpuss face.
Katy cracked a coconut.
We tried a little taste.

We do a lot of show and tell,
but none where we all ate so well!

Careers

We made a list in homeroom class
of what we'd like to be.
There's no career we've studied yet
that has appeal for me.

Arthur likes to plan and draw,
he'll be an architect.
Annie cares for animals,
she plans to be a vet.

Pedro plays the piccolo,
like a promising musician.
Gabriel gives speeches well,
he'll be a politician.

Erin is very organized,
she loves to plan events.
Brigit hopes she'll someday
be elected president.

I've considered all my talents.
I'm pretty sure I've found,
my ideal occupation
is to be a circus clown!

Anyone Can Be a Poet

It's possible you don't yet know it
but inside you there is a poet.
Use poems to express feelings you have—
funny or angry or silly or sad.
Learn all you can about meter and rhyme.
Count all the syllables found in a line.
Assemble some paper, a pencil or two.
Get started! Write freely from your point of view!

Glasses

We had some tests at school today.
I learned my hearing's fine.
But I can't read the letter chart
below the middle line.

I see the chalkboard writing
if I squeeze my eyes and squint.
I hold a book up to my nose
or I can't read the print.

My mom made me an appointment
with our neighborhood optician.
It seemed we needed to remedy
my nearsighted condition.

I worried, would my friends make fun
when I go to my classes?
Heck no! 'Cause half the kids, it seemed,
showed up in brand new glasses!

Sleeper

"I don't understand,"
my mom said, amazed,
"how you sleep so soundly
on most school days.

"You're grouchy and grumpy,
not one bit enthused.
You hide under the blankets
and twice hit the snooze.

"I flip on the lights,
and give you a shake.
My patience is thinning.
You're so hard to wake.

"But this morning is different.
It's now Saturday.
You're up right at daybreak
all ready to play!"

The Dog Ate My Homework (Really!)

Our assignment was unusual.
We're going to celebrate
the day before Thanksgiving
with food the pilgrims ate.

I volunteered at once and said,
"I'll bring a pumpkin pie.
I'm sure they had dessert back then.
I'll give it one good try."

My mom gave me instructions:
"To prepare it right you must
knead the dough and roll it out
to make a flaky crust."

I mixed a can of pumpkin
along with other stuff.
We baked it in the oven
'til Mom said, "It's done enough."

We put it on the counter
then I went to play.
The dog then ate my homework,
just like the old cliché.

My mom went out and bought a pie,
and I was quite relieved.
I told the truth at school that day,
but no one would believe!

Lousy Middle Name

To take the roll, my teacher asked
to share our full names with the class.
First name, last, and middle too…
She looked at me, "I'll start with you."

I sputtered out my first, then last,
hoping she would let it pass.
I couldn't speak, my tongue went numb.
My middle name is really dumb!

I stared real hard down at the floor.
I wished I could slip out the door.
I choked and gasped and hung my head.
My cheeks were turning very red.

A sweat broke out. My hands were shaking.
"Such a long time you are taking!"
I turned to face her, so ashamed.
Then blurted out my middle name.

The class all laughed, the teacher roared.
She'd never heard that name before.
She said, at last, when she could speak,
"Well, I admit, that one's unique."

Sadly, it's not Rhett or Barry,
Pedro, Pete, Levi, or Larry,
Johnny, Jason, Tevin, Todd,
Abraham, or just plain Bob!

There's ninety names I could have had.
Mine's only used when Mom is mad.
Go ahead, now, try to guess.
the name that causes me such stress!

Whatever

When I was just born, my mom asked my dad,
"Do you like the name Nicholas Trevor?"
My father, not paying attention at all,
responded, "Oh well, dear…whatever."

But Mom was persistent, and so tried again,
"Nicholas Kevin sounds clever.
Or maybe Nick Phillip or Peter or Paul."
My dad said, "I like, ummmm…whatever."

My poor distraught mother was getting nowhere.
"Can't you come up with anything better?"
My dad shrugged his shoulders, and offered no help,
and retorted again, "Well…whatever."

"Last chance," she fumed, "I'm not kidding at all.
 A nice middle name, now or never."
No answer was offered, and so I became
officially Nicholas…Whatever.

CHAPTER FOUR

Siblings

Old Fuzzy

Clair won't take a nap,
and she won't go to bed,
unless her fuzzy blanket
is right next to her head.

It's really worn and badly torn
but just can't be replaced.
She holds onto that silky edge
and rubs it on her face.

The fabric is unravelling,
the color's badly faded.
Mom tried a brand new substitute
but Clair won't be persuaded.

But we've all loved our fuzzies
and we won't interfere.
With time that soft old blanket
will simply disappear.

What Will She Wear?

A tank top, a tutu, a princess tiara,
a much-too-small hand-me-down shirt…
Pink plaid pajamas or plum purple tights,
all paired with my old T-ball shirt.
She won't care a bit
if her clothes do not fit,
but it's likely my young sister Clair
will wear one cowgirl boot
with her own birthday suit,
and choose to be otherwise bare!

Just a Phase

My sister had some friends to stay.
I counted three or four.
It's not polite to eavesdrop,
still, I listened through the door.

It's called a slumber party,
but no one goes to bed.
I stayed real still and tried to hear
the weird things that they said…

"My dad won't see my point of view.
I tried to get a new curfew.
Is that a pimple that I saw?
I think I need a push-up bra.
I'm so alone without a phone.
This make-up makes me look so grown.
My clothes are just so out of style.
My parents treat me like a child.
My hormones seem to fluctuate.
When will I be allowed to date?

My mother says she never will
let me wear a two-inch heel.
Have you heard that new boy band?
My parents just don't understand."

They ordered out for pizza.
And talked all through the night
Then restyled one another's hair,
and had a pillow fight.

They all left in the morning
with eyes all red and glazed.
"Thankfully," my mom told Dad,
"It's just a pre-teen phase."

Terrible Twos

Who says "No!" when she means "Yes?"
Shakes her head? Holds her breath?
Mom and Dad, what should we do
about this kid who just turned two?

She throws her toys and stomps her feet.
The dog and kitten both retreat.
I don't remember being two
but these are things I'd never do.

But my parents, now, are not alarmed.
"We've had two kids, we've been forewarned.
Another year, and we'll be through
forever with the Terrible Twos."

My Sister's Diary

I told my best friend Gary
"We only have a minute
to find my sister's diary
and read everything that's in it."

We hoped for shocking details,
but much to our frustration,
it was just a bunch of boring stuff,
no juicy revelation.

My sister Sue is sneaky.
She slinked in like a bandit.
"I'm going to tell our mom right now.
I've caught you both red-handed."

Now I have to do her chores,
and I'm forever grounded.
The diary wasn't worth one dime
I wish we'd never found it!

Weapons of Massive Destruction

I went to the store, bought a new marker set,
some bold and bright colors I hadn't used yet.
I usually keep them in small plastic bins,
with all of my crayons and pencils and pens.
But my friends Max and Gary came over to play.
I failed to put all of my markers away.
Clearly forgetting the times I've been told
to keep things such as these from a small two-year-old.

In no time at all, the living room walls
were covered in scribbles and doodles and scrawls.
Clair could hardly resist the temptation
to borrow my markers for her own creation.
I scrubbed and I rubbed as I cleaned it real good.
Would it come off? I hoped that it would!
I had paid no attention to Mom's clear instruction
to put away weapons of massive destruction.

Who Needs Toys?

My sister has a play room
that's filled with all her toys—
Puzzles, blocks, a horse that rocks,
but none that she enjoys.

She'd rather bang on pans and pots,
or write on all the walls,
or unroll toilet tissue
than play with any dolls.

She had a birthday party
with presents wrapped and tied.
She opened each and every one
then threw the gifts aside.

She wadded up the paper,
built the boxes in a stack.
She clearly doesn't want them.
They should take those presents back.

(And swap for something that I'd like…
perhaps a brand new racing bike!)

The Way She Was

My sister Sue and her friend Sarah
bought some shadow and mascara.
Then asked my mom if they could use
lipstick and her bright red rouge.

They spent an hour up in her room.
When all was done, I just assumed
they'd look a whole lot better then.
But, oh boy, was I wrong again!

They both appeared, it seemed to me,
like zombies from a bad movie.
Is this sister really mine?
She more resembles Frankenstein.

"You look nice," my parents told her.
"Save it 'til you're much, much older."
But Sue gave me a hug because
I said she's fine the way she was.

Death of the V-neck

My sister did the laundry,
my clothes no longer stink,
but she mixed the whites with all the brights
and my underwear is pink.

She used too much detergent.
The suds were overflowing
on the floor and out the door.
Still the washer kept on going.

The rinsing took forever.
Then came a violent spin.
She took out clothes that looked no more
like the ones that she put in.

My shirts all lost their buttons.
No sock can find a mate.
I won't be wearing one matched pair.
But still I'm feeling great!

She did me quite a favor.
She made my life much better
I have her to thank because she shrank
That AWFUL, TERRIBLE, PLEASE-DON'T-
    MAKE-ME-WEAR-IT-EVER-AGAIN…
V-necked sweater!
(Sorry Grandma!)

CHAPTER FIVE

Mishaps and Misadventures

Bad Medicine

This medicine's awful,
it tastes like dirt,
and I just can't believe
it will heal where I hurt.

Is this, now, the very best
cure I can take
for a fast-spreading flu
and a bad stomach ache?

My head is now throbbing.
This rash is much redder.
A green gooey syrup
won't make it much better.

I whine and I cry,
and I act quite bad.
My mother is getting
a little bit mad.

She asks, "How else, nurse,
can you treat this infection?"
He says, with a grin,
"With a great big injection!"

Scary Movie, Scary Dreams

A scary movie's on TV.
It's one I just can't wait to see.
There's monsters, mummies, guts and gore,
bodies, blood, and so much more.

"Bad idea," my mother says.
"You'll have nightmares in your bed."
I sneek in Sue's room—while she's gone—
and turn that awful movie on.

I tell myself, "These things aren't real."
But they were pretty scary, still.
I try so hard to watch it but
it's tough to see when my eyes are shut!

My hair's on end. My nerves are shot.
Who's to blame? Well, it's all my fault.
Mom is always right, it seems.
I can't stop having scary dreams!

A Nap? Are You Kidding?

Take a nap? Are you kidding?
What on earth for?
I'm in second grade.
I don't nap anymore!

Naps are for babies,
and grandparents too.
I can't take a nap,
I've got too much to do.

I'll pick up my clothes,
might make up my bed.
I'll play with my sister
and get my pets fed.

I'll finish my homework
before I forget.
Then work on my project
that's not quite done yet.

So don't think I'm tired
though I stayed up past ten.
I watched monster movies
and couldn't sleep then.

But, wait a bit, just
before I start moving,
I'll rest for a minute.
But soon I am snooozzzzzzing.

Freckles

They're sprinkled on my nose
and spread across my cheeks.
Five or ten appear again
once or twice a week.

Spots look good on cheetahs,
but not so good on me.
I'd like to wake up just one day
and find I'm freckle-free.

But Grandma loves my freckles,
each and every one.
She said that they are kisses
she sent me from the sun.

What's the Secret?

I'll tell you a secret.
I hope you will keep it.
Button your lip.
You can't let it slip.
Hide it real well.
Don't ever tell.
Wait! Now I need it.
Please can you repeat it?
Oh no, is it true?
You've forgotten it too?

Leaving Before Freezing

"Hurry, guys, c'mon, let's go.
It's the first day we've had any snow."
School was cancelled we were told.
Can't wait for buses in the cold.
A little chill can't keep away
my friends and I who want to play.
"If you're sledding now," my mother said,
"Wear gloves on your hands and a hat on your head.
It's a long walk, boys, remember please,
come home before you start to freeze."

We bundle up and run outside,
pulling tubes and sleds to ride.
It is about a half mile 'til
we reach our favorite sledding hill.
Coasting fast, racing down,
we slip and slide and spin around.
We tumble off, all laughing while
we get untangled from the pile.
My toes and nose are getting numb,
but I can't stop. It's too much fun.

How many times have I been told
be careful when you get too cold?
It's getting late and really frigid.
I've frozen each and every digit.

I wish I had considered leaving
way before I started freezing.
The fun we had was worth it all,
but I wonder, will I ever thaw?

One Illness or Another

I didn't study, not at all.
I'm going to fail my test.
What will I use for my excuse?
I'll make one up, I guess.

I planned to study early,
so I set my own alarm,
but as I reached to turn it off,
I fell and broke my arm.

I'm really wracked with rickets,
and itching from the scabies.
A mad dog took a bite of me,
so I've contracted rabies.

I ran into a doorway,
and got a bloody nose.
I couldn't put my shoes on,
there's a fungus on my toes.

I'm miserable with measles,
all covered up in spots.
I just might not recover
from a case of chickenpox.

I'm sick with cabin fever.
I suffer from neurosis.
I'm too weak to brush my teeth,
I now have halitosis.

I'll let my teacher choose between
one illness or another.
I'll be okay if through the day
she doesn't call my mother.

Step on a Crack

All the kids say, "Just beware.
You'll fall right through to who knows where.
If you must, let others pass,
or walk right on the nearby grass.
Take one step over, two steps back,
but never step on a sidewalk crack."

I walked around our cul-de-sac.
On purpose, stepped on every crack.
There was no awful tragedy,
the whole earth did not swallow me,
and I report that, thankfully,
I'm not a sidewalk casualty.

Allergies

A runny nose,
and red-rimmed eyes...
it's springtime now
and no surprise.
I'm sneezing, wheezing
for good reason.
Ah-choo! It's the start
of allergy season.

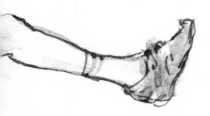

Bad Ice Cream Choice

One hot and humid August day
my sister asked, politely, "May
we walk down to the Dairy Freeze,
and have an ice cream, Grandma, please?"

"Just one serving, not too large."
My sister Sue was put in charge.
I thought I'd get a waffle cone,
but Sue said in her bossy tone…

"To have it in a cup is best.
You won't have all the sloppy mess."
But I ignored her sound advice,
and shortly after, paid the price.

It wasn't long before the scoop
transitioned into chocolate soup.
My ice cream formed a steady drip
and dribbled down my lower lip.

It then continued on my shirt
and dropped in plops onto the dirt.
A cold and sticky melted ooze
was forming in my tennis shoes.

To now enjoy this ice cream treat,
I'll have to lick it off my feet.

Climb Too High

Sometime in the afternoon
on the twenty-second day of June,
my friend unwisely follows me
as I climb up the apple tree.

It seems as good as it can get.
We don't see that the sun has set.
Way up in the highest limb,
we can't descend in this strong wind.

It's raining now and we're marooned.
We better get some help and soon!
My mom had always specified,
"Don't climb too late or climb too high."

She has to call authorities.
They seem a tiny bit displeased.
Our nosy neighbors gather 'round.
The cherry picker brings us down.

I'm now not fond of apple trees.
My punishment is raking leaves!

Heroes in Disguise

My mom said my buddies can come over soon.
Gary was helping me clean up my room.
We picked up the clothes, and put out the trash.
We were finally finished, and then Gary asked,
"Why keep these stuffed things? They look pretty rough.
Can't we throw them out? They've been here long enough."

I looked at my pals that I've had all these years.
Ted was distraught. Bear was in tears.
Ge rid of them now? I won't! That's for sure!
But to keep them forever might seem immature.
I don't want my buddies to make fun of me.
My Bear and my Ted—what else could they be?
I had an idea. "How about it, you guys?
I'll dress you each up in a hero disguise!"

April First

"What's with you today?" my friend Gary asked.
"Your freckles are faded. You've got a heat rash.
There's rocks in your socks. Both shoes do not match.
On the back of your head, there's a large tick attached.
I see hairy warts grow on two of your toes,
and a large juicy booger just left of your nose.
Those pants have a hole, your underwear shows.
It looks like you're wearing my sister's old clothes."

What else could go wrong? Must this get much worse?
"I fooled you!" said Gary, "Today's April first!"

Things I'll Never Do Again

Counting now, from one to ten,
things I'll never do again:

Use some worms for fishing bait.
Guess my Grandma's age or weight.
Score on the opponent's side.
Take an escalator ride.
Pull my classmate's ponytail.
Assume my gerbil is a male.
Stay out late in freezing weather.
Wear that awful V-necked sweater.
Read my sister's diary.
Blame the dog for gas from me!

CHAPTER SIX

At Our House

Clean Up a Fortune

I must clean my room.
It's really a mess.
But where to get started
is anyone's guess.

Here's library books
with due dates long past,
some science assignments
I need for my class.

I found some stale peanuts
and old pizza crusts,
A half-eaten candy bar,
covered in dust…

A watch that has stopped,
crayons that are broken,
some ribbon and wrapping,
a Chuck E Cheese token.

I work my way slowly
to clean up the pile.
It's clear that I haven't
picked up in a while.

But wait! At the bottom
I look really hard.
Here's two dollar bills,
a toy store gift card…

A coupon for ice cream,
a pack of new gum.
I'll enjoy all these treats
when my cleaning is done.

I am pretty darned pleased
with my newly found fortune.
Remind me I must
clean my room much more often!

Where's the Frigidaire?

Where did we hide the Frigidaire?
Is that in the kitchen where
I don't see a space to spare?
There's stuff on magnets everywhere!

We've covered it from top to floor
with fifty coupons (maybe more)
that Mom will use when shopping for
our family at the grocery store.

There's special sales on deli meats
and remedies for ticks and fleas,
big savings on pimento cheese—
purchase three, next one's free.

Pork chops from the butcher's mart,
return receipt from auto parts,
Clair's display of kiddie art,
a homemade Valentine's Day heart.

Maybe sooner, maybe later,
we'll locate that refrigerator.

Mac and Cheese

Looking for the perfect food?
One that's uniformly good?
Take a vote, I guarantee
the winner will be mac and cheese.

One small plate is not enough.
I'll eat it 'til I'm truly stuffed.
I'll try a turnip, choke down peas,
if both are served with mac and cheese.

School lunch is hit or miss.
Some hate that and some like this.
But every kid in class agrees
you can't go wrong with mac and cheese.

Stuff on the Stairs

Mom stared at the pile of stuff on the stairs.
Everyone puts all their upstairs stuff there.
We're too lazy to walk to the very next floor.
Stuff piles up quickly as we add some more.

Our book bags, our toys, our towels for the bath
were gathered alongside a small narrow path.
The pile it created was seven feet high.
if more stuff is added it could reach the sky.

Despite just how often our mother had pleaded,
we never listened—her words went unheeded.
But, gosh, we regretted what would happen next
while she bravely attempted a climb up the steps…

All our possessions we stacked carelessly
rumbled and roared as the pile was set free.
Consequently, that evening, at quarter 'til five,
an avalanche buried our mother alive!

Ice Cream Remedy

I had a tonsillectomy.
The nurses come to check on me.
I can't speak now with this sore throat.
Just like a frog, I only croak.
The situation's really dire.
Every swallow feels like fire.
I whispered what I need to heal
is ice cream for my every meal.

Pile It on the Pie

What can I put on a pizza?
How much can I pile on that pie?
I'll start with some meat on a crust made of wheat
and build this thing nine inches high!
Then toss on some sausage or bacon or ham,
with onions and olives and cheese.
I'll pick pepperoni or maybe baloney.
But add some anchovies? No, please!
I might get creative and mix artichokes
with sauerkraut, cucumbers, or kale.
I'll ask my friend Gary to bring calamari
or maybe a small lobster tail.
It's done in the oven, we're ready to eat.
We don't need a fork or a spoon.
But we've already learned that we'll suffer a burn
if we sample our pizza too soon!

Dozens of Cousins

My mom has seven sisters,
my dad has three or four.
And one or the other
has two older brothers.
I just can't keep up anymore.

Last week we had a reunion.
They came from near and far.
I had fun with my cousins—
there's dozens and dozens.
I hope they come back every year.

Dream of a Sitter

A babysitter who I'd like
would always let me ride my bike
through the house and down the stairs
into the yard where I find there's…

A trampoline she bought for me,
a tire swing in the apple tree,
a cake she's baked that's really good,
and ice cream for the neighborhood.

There's ponies for us all to ride,
a gym set with a ten-foot slide.
I'm everybody's favorite friend,
but, sadly, soon my dream will end.

It wasn't real, but all the same,
I'll try to find that sitter's name!

Best Friends

Today my friend Gary was over to play.
He told me some sad news—he might move away.
We're always together, we make a great twosome.
We thought very hard to find a solution.

Would Mom really notice one little kid more?
We have just three kids; he'd make only four.
Gary and I have a wonderful option.
Maybe our family should try to adopt him!

CHAPTER SEVEN

Grandma and Grandpa II

Yard Sale Tradition

Grandpa and I, on a serious mission,
go shopping on weekends—our yard sale tradition.
We start when it's dark. He wakes me at six.
(If you don't arrive early, you won't get good picks.)

There's well-worn tools to contemplate:
a punctured hose and rusty rake,
a croquet set, a wooden box
with nuts and bolts, keys and locks.
And what a find! A singing Elvis
on a canvas made of velvet.
And finally, a missing part
for Grandpa's motorbike to start.

We load up when we have enough,
and show Grandma our yard sale stuff.
She just sighs, "I understand,
your grandpa is the Fix-It Man!"

Debate with Weight

Gramps and I were reading poems.
Grandma was next to him.
He said, "My dear, your dress is nice.
It makes you look quite slim."

tools
$12

"Well, thanks, I guess," Grandma replied.
"Should I interpret that
you're saying, in my other clothes,
I must look somewhat fat?"

"Oh honey, no," Grandpa went on.
"I think you look just great.
I hadn't even noticed that
you've put on a little weight."

Grandma, now, was all incensed.
"Explain a bit more, please.
It seems you're implicating
that I'm morbidly obese."

"Well, heavens no," he blundered,
uneasy and red-faced.
"It's not so bad. I still can get
my arms around your waist."

The more my grandpa tried to say,
the further things went south.
There's no debate about Grandma's weight.
It's best to shut your mouth!

Grandma.com

Grandma's in computer class.
"I'll not be left behind.
I like to keep my senses sharp,
and activate my mind.

"I'll take on new technology.
I'll learn to interface,
to download, upload, scan, and Skype,
to bookmark, cut, and paste."

She budgets on her spread sheet,
shops now on Amazon.
Grandma's in her own domain.
She's mastered all dot-com.

Recycle, Please

I kicked a can, then smashed it up,
and tossed it in the trash.
"Is there not a better place
to put it?" Grandpa asked.

"You might have thrown that can away,
but it's not forever gone.
It ends up in a landfill
where garbage will live on.

"A can will be recycled,
turned into something new.
If we all participate, it makes
a cleaner world for you."

Grandma Rocks

Grandma found her saddle shoes
and laced them over bobby sox.
She dusted off her phonograph.
"C'mon kids, time to rock!
We'll shake things up right from the start.
Let's loosen every body part.
Follow me and shake your wrist.
Turn this way, that way. Do the Twist."
Grandma danced a wild Watusi.
Watch out now! She's getting whoozy!

Grandpa joined our party then.
"I still can cut a rug!"
He wore his high school jacket—
though it seemed a bit too snug.
    "Here's my favorite. Are you ready?
      Flap your arms and do the Freddie."
        He held his nose. "I'll jump right in,
          And teach you how to do the Swim!"

            They lined us up all in a row.
              We'll slow it down and do the Stroll.
                Mom and Dad, our neighbors, too
                  recalled the songs that they all knew.
                    We danced to every single one.
                      Boy! The sixties seemed like fun!

Workshop Helper

Grandpa's in his workshop where
I help him build and make repairs.
I pay attention to the rules,
especially with his power tools.

We find essentials Grandpa stashes:
hard hats, belts, our safety glasses.
Then organize the things we'll use:
nails and rivets, nuts and screws.

I learn a lot of workman skills,
how to hammer, saw, and drill.
He always offers this advice:
"Cut just once but measure twice.
And don't forget, that in the end,
duct tape is a man's best friend."

My Hero

Memorial Day...
the band played loudly.
There with his buddies,
my grandpa walked proudly.
He carried the flag,
his eyes straight ahead.
"It's important for us
to remember," he said.
He scanned the formation
of planes in the sky,
saluted successors,
with tears in his eyes.
"My father before me,
and his father, too,
all served with honor.
It's just what we do.
We were not heroes,"
he said resolutely,
"We just did our job.
We just did our duty."

Grandpa's Rules

There's a lot of rules on Grandma's list,
but Grandpa thought of some she missed:

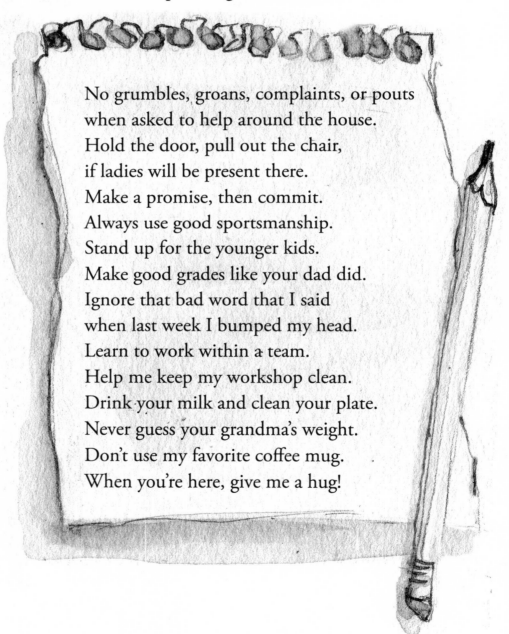

No grumbles, groans, complaints, or pouts
when asked to help around the house.
Hold the door, pull out the chair,
if ladies will be present there.
Make a promise, then commit.
Always use good sportsmanship.
Stand up for the younger kids.
Make good grades like your dad did.
Ignore that bad word that I said
when last week I bumped my head.
Learn to work within a team.
Help me keep my workshop clean.
Drink your milk and clean your plate.
Never guess your grandma's weight.
Don't use my favorite coffee mug.
When you're here, give me a hug!

Saved by the Gas

Every other Saturday,
my grandma's friends bring cards to play.
They drink hot tea and eat cold pasta.
Then settle down and play canasta.
It seems I hear a lot of chatter
'bout lots of things I don't think matter.

I don't get a chance to speak.
They pat my head and pinch my cheek.
They talk about their grandkids some,
and all the silly things we've done.
They trade their stories and compare us.
Meanwhile I get more embarrassed.

Oh great, Grandma, really swell!
She told about the pony "tale."
Boy, I wish I wasn't there.
She mentioned my pink underwear.
Before I could make my retreat
she described my ice cream feet.

They planned to stay all afternoon,
but suddenly fled from the room.
Each grabbed her coat, her hat, and purse,
and quickly started to disperse.

I was so very much relieved
when the last one ran to leave.
Grandpa chuckled, then he asked,
"Aren't you glad my dog passed gas?"

Night Time Hug

"How are you tonight?" I ask,
"Feel a little better?"
My grandpa answers, "Still," he says,
"A bit under the weather."

I think of how to cheer him up,
then climb a stool to look
atop the shelf too high for Clair,
so I can reach this book.

We laugh about my ice cream feet
and made-up babysitter.
Who'd of thought I'd eat a fly,
or raise a gerbil litter?

I read to him for half an hour.
We finish just past eight.
Grandpa's nodding off a bit.
"Well, Nick, it's getting late."

"I really love my time with you.
Tomorrow we'll read more."
I hug him extra hard tonight,
then gently close the door.

INDEX OF POEMS